Copyright: © Daniel Turner

ISBN-13: 978-1494356125

ISBN-10: 1494356120

All rights reserved. No part of this publication may be reproduced, stored in or introduced into a retrieval system, or transmitted in any for or by any means (electronic, mechanical, by photocopying, recording or otherwise) without the prior written permission of the author.

Part of the Simple guide series

SIMPLE HISTORY
A SIMPLE GUIDE TO
WORLD WAR I
1914 - 1918

Written and Illustrated by
Daniel Turner

CONTENTS

Introduction	5
The beginning of WWI	6
What were the causes of WWI?	7
Zeppelin raids	8
Christmas truce	9
Conscription	10
Weapons & technology	11
Battle of the Somme	12
Trench cross-section	14
Rations	15
Russian Revolution	16
Uniforms & equipment	17
Aerial combat	18
End of the war	20
Leaders of WWI - The Treaty of Versailles	21
The Great War statistics	22
Remembrance	23
Glossary	24
Index	25

INTRODUCTION

The Great War or the First World War (there is a sequel!) was a war of epic proportions. It started from a simple assassination, but there is more to it than that. Competing nations, mass produced weapons and big armies made Europe a tinder box ready to explode!

In 1914 with war declared, most people couldn't wait to seek glory. By 1918 when the war was finally over, the world never wanted to see such a global conflict ever again...

THE BEGINNING OF WWI   1914

On June 28th, 1914 Archduke Franz Ferdinand was assassinated in Sarajevo by Gavrilo Princip, a member of the Serbian 'Black Hand'. Franz Ferdinand was an important figure in the Austro-Hungarian empire, and the Black Hand wanted their country of Bosnia-Herzegovina to be separate from the empire.

TRIPLE ENTENTE   **CENTRAL POWERS**

Britain

Germany

VS

France

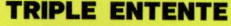
Austro-Hungary

Russia

Ottoman Empire

To teach them a lesson, Austria declared war on Serbia with Germany's support. Because different countries had treaties with each other, they soon started to declare war on their enemies. Russia and France declared war on Germany, and Germany declared war on France making Britain declare war on Germany. Soon there were two teams, the 'Triple Entente' VS 'The Central Powers'.

WHAT WERE THE CAUSES OF WWI?

Imperialism

The British empire spanned over 1/4 of the earth by 1900! Colonies such as Australia, New Zealand and India were owned by Britain and made her very powerful.

Germany also wanted an empire, targeting Africa for colonies. Most of Africa had been claimed by Britain and France, so Germany's interests caused tensions.

Arms race

Many nations in Europe had built up huge armies and weapons in preparation for a large scale war. The 'naval race' (competing to have the largest naval ships) between Britain and Germany, created tensions between each other.

Alliances

Fearing their neighbours, Germany, Austria and Italy formed a triple alliance promising to help each other if one of them was attacked. Britain, France and Russia likewise formed their own alliance.

Mobilised forces 1914 -1918

Russia	12,000,000
Germany	11,000,000
Great Britain	8,905,000
France	8,410,000
Austria-Hungary	7,800,000
Italy	5,615,000
United States	4,355,000
Ottoman Empire	2,850,000
Bulgaria	1,200,000

ZEPPELIN RAIDS — 1914-1915

Germany had 'The Schlieffen plan' - because it was scared of fighting France in the west and Russia in the east. The idea was to quickly defeat France then focus on Russia. But this meant that Germany had to invade neutral Belgium to get to France. The war had begun...

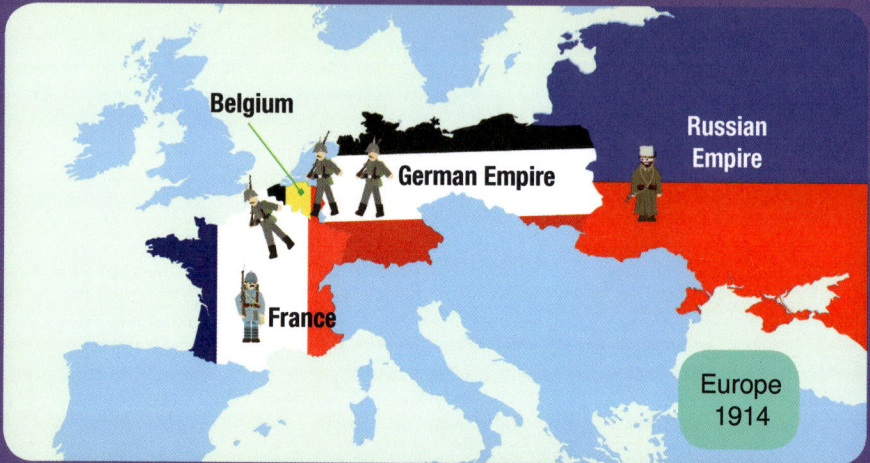

In 1915 Germany starts using Zeppelin bombing raids on Britain.

CHRISTMAS TRUCE, DECEMBER, 1914

On Christmas 1914, German and British soldiers put down their weapons and made a temporary truce.

Trading cigarettes and chocolate was common

Soldiers sang Christmas carols together

The dead and wounded were allowed to be carried back

British & German soldiers played football

MERRY CHRISTMAS!

1914

CONSCRIPTION   1916

In January 1916, Britain started to introduce conscription. Men who didn't volunteer earlier were made to enlist into the army.

The battle of Verdun begins, fought between the French and German armies. It was one of the bloodiest and longest battles of the war.

WEAPONS & TECHNOLOGY OF WWI

Mark I tank

The Tank

The British designed the tank as a response to the problem of trench warfare. The first tanks were very crude and broke down a lot, but these armoured vehicles were soon copied by all the fighting countries with devastating results.

Poison Gas

An absolutely deadly weapon. Chlorine gas was first used at the battle of Ypres in 1915, and mustard gas was used later in the war. If you were hit by a gas attack you would suffocate and choke before falling dead. The solution was to quickly put on a protective mask or wee into a rag and put it against your mouth!

Vickers machine gun
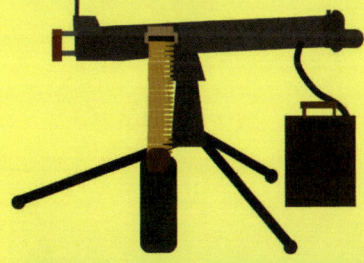

Sopwith Camel

The Machine gun

The cause of millions of casualties in the war, the machine-gun could shoot hundreds of rounds per minute. Because of the flawed tactic of charging head on at the enemy trench, the machine-gun could often cut down entire armies.

Biplanes

At the start of the war, planes were used for scouting but as the war developed they were used as fighters and bombers. A biplane is named for having two set of wings.

11

THE BATTLE OF THE SOMME, 1916

Artillery fire from cannons could kill a soldier before he even had a chance to get to the enemy trench.

Tanks made good cover for troops, and would scare the enemy, too bad they broke down half the time!

British soldiers were ordered to charge at the machine gun fire! A bad strategy.

Most soldiers on both sides would carry a rifle.

The Lewis gun, a portable machine gun.

Barbed wire trapped advancing soldiers, if they were unlucky to get caught in it

TRENCH CROSS-SECTION

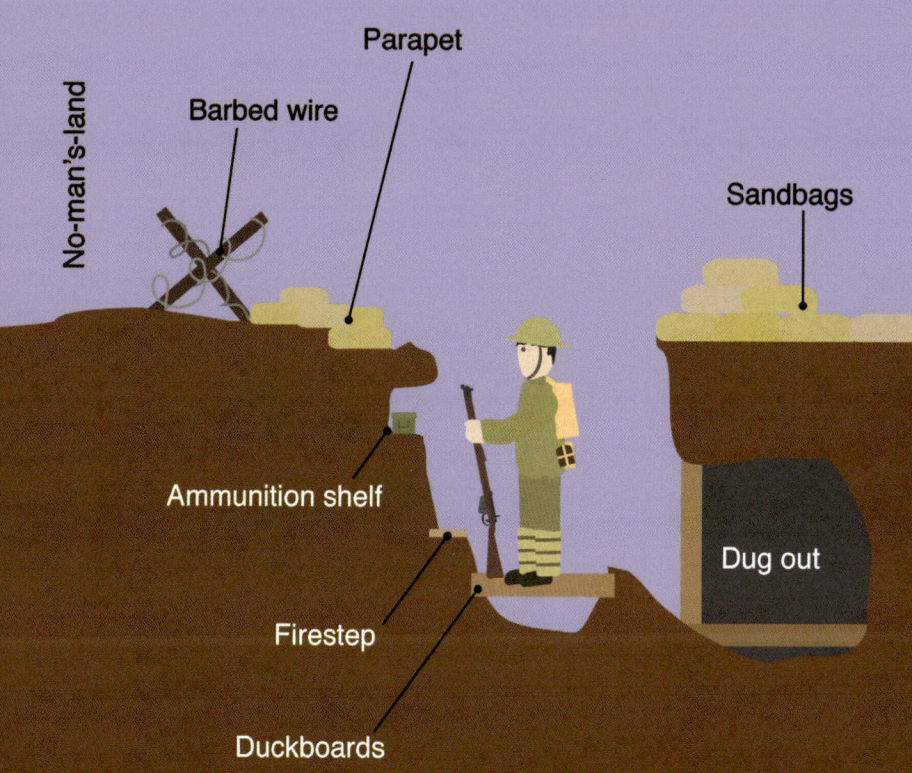

Very early on in the war, both sides dug out trenches so that they would not lose any ground. Living in a trench was a horrible experience as they were damp, muddy, full of disease and constantly bombed by enemy artillery. Trenches were dug in a zigzag pattern so that if the enemy entered it, he could not shoot straight down the line.

 **RUSSIAN REVOLUTION** **1917**

Losing the war, Germany launches an unrestricted submarine warfare campaign. Attacking American ships bringing food and supplies to Britain caused America to join the war against Germany.

Tsar Nicholas II abdicates. The Russian revolution starts the Bolshevik government led by Lenin. Russia deserts the war effort and signs a pact with Germany promising they will not attack each other.

UNIFORMS & EQUIPMENT

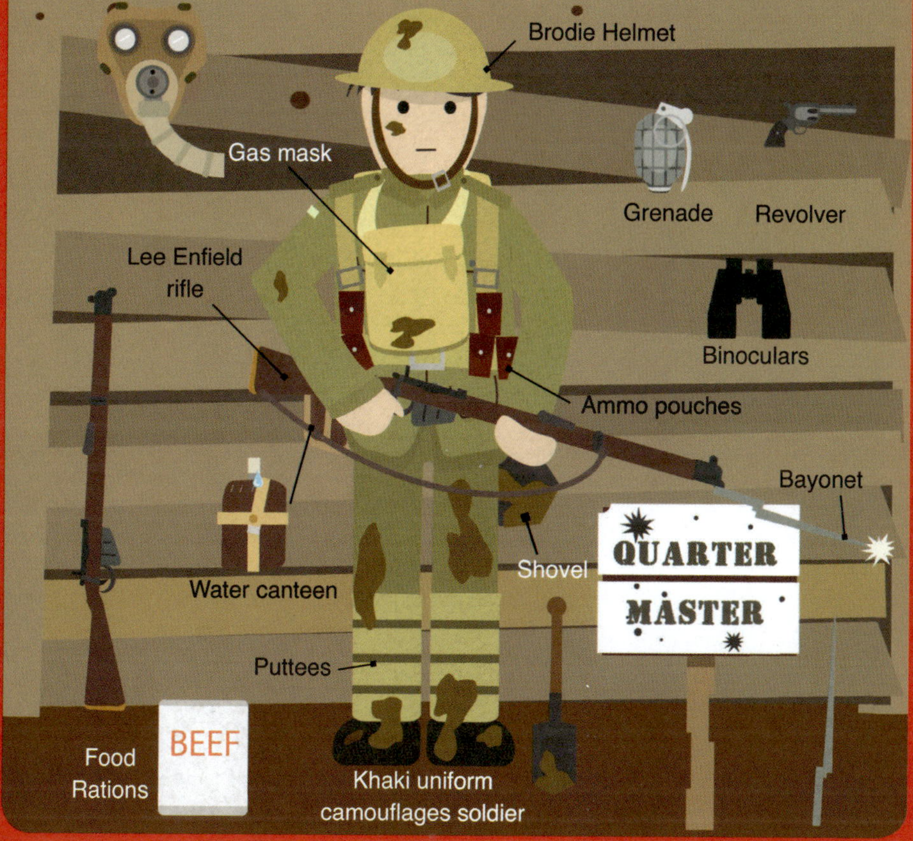

- Brodie Helmet
- Gas mask
- Lee Enfield rifle
- Grenade
- Revolver
- Binoculars
- Ammo pouches
- Bayonet
- Water canteen
- Shovel
- QUARTER MASTER
- Puttees
- Food Rations
- BEEF
- Khaki uniform camouflages soldier

British | French | Russian | German soldier & pilot

Uniforms were coloured in drab shades to camouflage soldiers into their environment (although French uniforms were blue, not much use!)

AERIAL COMBAT

The earliest use of planes were for scouting out enemy positions. As the war progressed, both the Allied and Central Powers mounted machine guns on their aircraft, creating deadly dogfights in the skies. The most famous flying ace was Manfred von Richthofen or the 'Red Baron' who shot down 80 enemy aircraft!

Flying aces were celebrated as modern knights.

18

THE END OF THE WAR — 1918

Germany and the Central Powers lose the war. Germany's leader Kaiser Wilhelm II abdicates.
The armistice was signed on November 11th of the 11th hour ending the war.

What next?
As a result Germany signs the 'Treaty of Versailles' in 1919 and is severely punished.

LEADERS OF WWI, THE TREATY OF VERSAILLES

ANGRY ← → HAPPY

Punish Germany!

Peace.

Prime Minister Georges Clemenceau
France

France had been devastated by Germany. Clemenceau wanted to punish the country severely. He wanted Germany to pay reparations (money) to fix the damage.

Prime Minister David Lloyd George
Britain

The damage done to Britain was less severe by Germany. David Lloyd George was also afraid of the new threat of Communist Russia, so did not want to punish Germany as much as France wanted to.

President Woodrow Wilson
USA

The USA was the least affected by the war, and saw itself as the peace maker. Woodrow Wilson had 14 points promoting peace by banning secret treaties and letting nations be free from empires.

THE GREAT WAR STATISTICS

The First World War which people thought would be over by Christmas, lasted for 4 years. It had killed millions, and destroyed nations.

28 JULY 1914 – 11 NOVEMBER 1918

OF THE 65 MILLION MEN DEPLOYED TO FIGHT

50% WERE KILLED OR WOUNDED

WWI TOTAL CASUALTIES

MILITARY CASUALTIES: 9,720,000
CIVILIAN CASUALTIES: 8,870,000
MILITARY WOUNDED: 19,800,000

ALLIED CASUALTIES
TOTAL MILITARY DEATHS 5.7 MILLION

CENTRAL POWERS CASUALTIES
TOTAL MILITARY DEATHS 4.02 MILLION

FIRSTS:
TRENCH WARFARE
PLANES
TANKS
SUBMARINES
WIRELESS COMMUNICATION
POISONOUS GAS

FLYING ACES
- 80 KILLS - MANFRED VON RICHTHOFEN (THE RED BARON)
- 75 KILLS - RENÉ FONCK
- 61 KILLS - EDWARD MANNOCK

We remember the First World War with the poppy symbol because they grew on the bloody battlefields in the aftermath.

 # GLOSSARY

Abdicate
When a leader steps down from power.
Alliance
A agreement between two nations to fight together.
Artillery
Large cannons that shoot explosive shells onto the battlefield.
Armistice
A agreement to end the war.
Black Hand
Nickname for Serbian assassins.
Camouflage
A pattern or colour that disguises a soldier with his surroundings.
Central Powers
Germany, Austro-Hungary and Turkey.
Colony
A country part of an empire.
Conscription
When people are made to enlist into the army.
Imperialism
When a powerful nation, takes over and owns colonies.

Mobilised
When a country's military is ready to go to battle.
Rations
A fixed amount of food for everyone during shortages.
Revolution
When people in a country change the current political system.
Treaty
An agreement between nations.
Trench
Long holes in the ground where soldiers lived and fought in.
Trench foot
A disease of the foot from being in damp trenches.
Triple Entente
Britain, France and Russian alliance.
Unrestricted submarine warfare
German navy policy to destroy supplies going to Britain.
Volunteer
Going to fight by choice.

INDEX

abdicate **20**
aircraft **11,18,19**,22
alliance **6,7,16**,21
artillery 12,13
armistice **20**,21

camouflage 17
Central Powers **6,7,8,16,18,20**
Christmas **9**
colony **7**
conscription **10**

David Lloyd George **21**

equipment **17**

Franz Ferdinand **6**

gas **11**,17
Georges Clemenceau **21**

Imperialism **7**

Kaiser Wilhelm II **16,20**

Lenin **16**

machine gun **11,12,13,18,19**

rations **15**
Red Baron **18,19**,22
remembrance **23**
Russian revolution **16**

statistics **22**

tank **11,12,13**
technology **11**
Treaty of Versailles **21**
trench warfare 9,**12,13,14**
Triple Entente **6**, **21**

uniform **17**

Verdun **10**

weapons **17**
Woodrow Wilson **21**

Zeppelin **8**,12,13

Printed in Great Britain
by Amazon